S0-AYB-270

2 84

WHEN A CHRISTIAN
AND A JEW MARRY

WHEN A CHRISTIAN AND A JEW MARRY

by Ronald Luka, C.M.F.

With a Jewish Perspective by
Rabbi Bernard M. Zlotowitz

PAULIST PRESS
New York / Paramus / Toronto

ACKNOWLEDGMENTS

Acknowledgment is herein made to the following for permission to quote from their copyrighted material:

McGraw-Hill Book Company, for material from THE EXPERIMENTAL LITURGY BOOK, edited by Robert Hoey. Copyright© 1969 by Herder & Herder, Inc. Used with permission.

International Committee on English in the Liturgy, Inc., for the English translation of the Rite of Marriage. Copyright © 1969 by International Committee on English in the Liturgy, Inc. All rights reserved.

Divine Word Publications, for material from THE MEANING OF LOVE AND MARRIAGE, by Alphonsus Jansen.

Confraternity of Christian Doctrine, for excerpts from THE NEW AMERICAN BIBLE, copyright © 1970. Used herein by permission of the Confraternity of Christian Doctrine, copyright owner.

Bruce Publishing Co., for material from SANCTUARY MANUAL, compiled by Rev. Walter Schmitz, S.S. Copyright © 1965 by Bruce Publishing Co.

Copyright © 1973 by
The Missionary Society
of St. Paul the Apostle
in the State of New York

Library of Congress
Catalog Card Number: 73-77393

ISBN 0-8091-1748-7

Published by Paulist Press
Editorial Office: 1865 Broadway, N.Y., N.Y. 10023
Business Office: 400 Sette Drive, Paramus, N.J. 07652

Printed and bound in the
United States of America

HQ1031
.L94
1973
6+s

Contents

I dedicate this work to the memory of a man I am proud to have been able to count as a friend and colleague, a sympathetic, compassionate, and understanding man who devoted the later years and final hours of his life to helping Christians and Jews begin a life of love together. May his memory long endure. Rabbi Samuel Halevi Baron.

Preface

When a man and woman marry, they begin a life of love together. As they do this, they need to find models and examples of love and understanding in their parents, in their clergymen, and in their religious communities. The love of couples entering interfaith marriages is under special stress. These couples have a special need to find these models of love and understanding. Often they find just the opposite.

In any marriage the partners have to adjust to the different attitudes, values, traditions, and outlooks on life that each of them has. When the parties are of different faiths this problem of adjustment is intensified.

For this reason, no marriage counselor would actively encourage interfaith marriages. This book does not intend to do so in principle either. It simply makes good sense to have as many bonds of unity going for a marriage beforehand as possible. Yet interfaith marriages have taken place and will continue to do so.

Clergymen, versed in the problems of marital adjustment, are also cautious about interfaith marriages. Among a few religious leaders, the whole subject is somewhat taboo. Some of these leaders may not welcome all of the ideas expressed in this book; this, of course, is their prerogative.

Yet the author has found the insights here expressed to be immensely helpful in premarital counseling. The people hurt by not having a frank, detailed, and open discussion of the liabilities and assets of interfaith marriages are the young couple involved. It is hoped that these observations in print might help many of these young couples, as well as their parents and religious leaders, in dealing with the question of interfaith marriage.

Our goal will be to minimize the liabilities associated with Christian-Jewish marriages and to maximize some of the unique assets that such a marriage may offer. When a special question or problem arises from the Catholic tradition, it will be earmarked as such. With encouragement or discouragement, Jews and Christians who have decided to marry will indeed marry. If they understand their situation as clearly as possible, their marriage may more clearly reflect the love of God for both these peoples.

I
To Mary and Irving

Caution: Faiths Crossing

If you're Jewish, find yourself a good Jewish girl or boy. If you're Christian, find yourself a good Christian girl or boy. That sounds so traditional that it's corny. But there is a lot of wisdom in the parents' traditional hope that their sons and daughters marry within their own faith.

During all of your married life you will be working to build a relationship of love with your partner. If you bring to the marriage common experiences you'll have a better chance of developing this relationship. Religion is only one of these areas of common experience. Race, social-economic background, educational level are others.

If a second grade dropout and a Ph.D. get married, they can anticipate a few extra difficulties in their married life. The same goes for a multimillionaire and a pauper, a black and a white, a Jew and a Christian. We're not concerned here with Church policy or the sensitivity of the Jewish community. We're strictly on the level of good marriage counseling sense.

Despite the fact that the percentage of marriage breakdown is higher for interfaith marriages than for marriages within the same faith, we are not saying

3

these marriages cannot develop into beautiful relationships. But we need to start off on a note of realism, especially in light of the fact that many couples preparing for marriage are high on idealism and low on realism. Let's hope that your love for each other is strong enough to surmount the additional stresses that will be placed upon it. It's more likely that you'll be able to work out a harmonious relationship if you realize, accept, and address yourself candidly to these difficulties before you say "I do."

No doubt the past few paragraphs didn't talk you out of getting married. They weren't intended to do that. If you're still playing the field, they were intended to offer some insight as to where you might look. A person shopping for a car with a family of nine kids is not too wise in looking at small compacts, nor is a person who earns a hundred a week too realistic in looking at brand new MG's. Your parents may never have read a marriage counseling book in their lives, but they knew what they were talking about when they encouraged you to go out with people of your own faith. Of course, this doesn't mean that we have to lock up all the Catholic kids for a dance in the church basement and maintain the local synagogue like a fortress. Fortunately we've gotten beyond the stage of Catholic and Jewish kids throwing rocks at each other. Respect, cooperation, friendship between these two groups are happily part of the climate of the day. But when considering a partner for marriage, see the blinking yellow light.

If you're immediately planning on marrying someone of another faith, we hope the rest of this book will provide insights as to how your marriage can be made as happy as possible. After stating this initial caution, we'll approach the whole question as positively as possible. You are actually in a great position to complement each other religiously. Through the sharing of your religious traditions you can have a more rather than less religious home. This very sharing can in fact bring you closer together.

On the Positive Side

Shared religious beliefs and practices help in building the foundations of a marriage. Jews and Christians share more beliefs than we usually think. Both believe in a God who created the world. Both believe that man has a special dignity in this created world. Both believe that God maintains a contact with this world he created; both are what we call theists. Both believe that our God maintains a loving contact with man. His love in both faiths is seen mirrored in the love of a lover for his beloved in the song of Solomon and even in the forgiving love of a husband for an unfaithful wife in the Book of Hosea. Both believe this a revealing God who in the Scriptures tells man something about himself, about man's relationship to him, and about man's relationship to his fellows. Both believe in a God who makes a covenant with man: an agreement to be faithful to us in spite of our unfaithfulness to him. Both believe this God promises a Savior who will rescue man from his unfaithfulness. Both believe man must worship and praise God by himself and in community with others. Both believe that Jesus, a Jew, was at least a great teacher who presented mankind with a high set of moral values and ideals. Both believe that the individual is supported by and adds his support to a community of believers, which among other things serves to guide him in making moral decisions. Both uphold similar ideals for marriage: that human sexuality is a wonderful gift from God, that the deepest physical expression of human love is authentically found only in marriage, that ideally men and women should live monogamous, permanent, and faithful unions as husbands and wives.

The emphasis on these common elements should not obscure the fact that there are major differences between Christians and Jews. However, differences do not have to be divisive; they can supplement the faith of each party. Here are some examples of how these faiths can supplement each other.

Most Christians are notoriously ignorant of God's workings with mankind before the coming of Jesus. What God has done with the people of Israel, he has done with the Christian community as well. Authentic Christianity has never seen itself as anything but Judaism plus. Everything that is part of the culture, the tradition, and the heritage of Israel is also part of the heritage of Christianity.

Furthermore, the rites of Judaism are much more closely associated with the home than those of present-day Christianity. In a Christian-Jewish marriage, the church, the temple, and the home all can supplement each other as focal points for prayer.

The Christian, on the other hand, can contribute to the Jew a knowledge and appreciation of the moral values and ideals of Jesus. His two great commandments of love of God and love of neighbor were taken from the Jewish Scriptures. He adds to this only his own example of how totally this love should be lived. The Christian is called not to give an abstract verbal testimony to this love, but to testify to it by his own love of

God, his spouse, his children, his in-laws, his neighbors and friends, especially those in great need.

Preparation in Faith

Often a young person approaching marriage does not have a very deep knowledge of or appreciation for his own faith. When he is marrying someone of the same faith, each might be able to make up for what the other lacks. However, the Christian marrying a Jew can hardly expect to get much of an appreciation for Christianity from his future spouse, nor can the Jew expect to get much of Judaism from the Christian. Each can and should give of his own religious tradition to the other, but he can hardly receive anything of his own tradition from one who does not share it with him. If the person lacks this knowledge of and appreciation for his own faith, he can hardly appreciate the religious bonds that can unite him with his future spouse, nor can he grasp the aspects of his faith that he can share with the other.

Frequently this lack of knowledge is intensified by an indifference or even a hostility toward their religious tradition. Hostility is often a by-product of lack of information or inaccurate information. One college chaplain commented to his students, "If I thought I had to believe all you think you have to believe, I'd be alienated from my religious tradition too."

Before a couple prepares for marriage they may well have to prepare for faith. The contact with a minister or priest and a rabbi prior to marriage may give them the opportunity not only to learn of each other's faiths, but to get a deeper grasp of their own as well. An understanding of and respect for both of these religious traditions will help them as they begin their marriage. They should seek out clergymen with whom they can explore any difficulties, doubts, uncertainties, and challenges they may wish to discuss. They may pick up some of the very worthwhile reading material which presents a summary of the beliefs and practices of their respective faiths, and both will read all the material.[1] As they read this material they should take the opportunity to jot down any questions they may have and discuss them with the clergymen preparing them for marriage.

Such reading and discussion will help them solve questions of faith, will help them appreciate their own religious tradition, and will better enable them to share as much of that tradition as possible with each other and with the children. They may have to look around a bit to find a clergyman with whom they can re-examine their faith, but it will certainly be worth the effort.

Some young people, fortunately very few, are so alienated from their religious tradition by the time they

[1]The following may be especially helpful: *Basic Judaism*, by Milton Steinberg (New York: Harcourt, Brace, Jovanovich); *What Is A Jew?* by Morris Kertzer (New York: Macmillan), and "Folkways and *Minhagim*," by Rabbi Bernard Zlotowitz, reprinted from *Keeping Posted* (New York: Union of American Hebrew Congregations). On Christianity, *A New Catechism* (New York: Herder and Herder) is fabulous. It's a translation of the Dutch Catechism and contains the very latest of theological and scriptural scholarship on an adult level. Catholics should not let the title scare them away. The book is not more of, "Who made you? God made you . . ." Again Catholics may find *Hangups in Religion*, by Ronald Luka, C.M.F. (Chicago: Claretian Publications) helpful. It explores many of the questions young Catholics are asking about their faith.

are ready for marriage that they are not even willing to do this re-examination, or even after this inquiry they come out totally hostile to their faith. These need to recognize that it is hypocritical and unauthentic for them to request a leader of their religious community to witness and bless their marriage. If one is totally alienated from the community of faith, he is better off accepting that fact and living with it, rather than inconsistently coming into contact with the believing community only at times of birth, marriage and death. The official presence of a religious leader at a wedding says something. It says that the couple consider their religious tradition important or are at least open to the faith community. The presence of these religious leaders is of deeper significance than the bouquets of flowers that might surround the altar. The religious leader is not just part of a nice backdrop for a beautiful day. Nor should these religious leaders be sought out just to keep parents and families happy. If the young person is totally alienated he should honestly accept this situation himself and confront his parents with the fact. A civil ceremony may be much more authentic in this situation.

Marriage is an excellent time for couples of the same faith or of different faiths to address themselves to the question of their religious commitment. Hopefully after exploration they can more firmly commit themselves to their community of faith. Otherwise they can make the decision to opt out of the community rather than just remaining a member in name.

A word of caution is, perhaps, needed here. Many young people are both very idealistic and very honest. They need to realize that none of us fully lives up to his religious ideals. We as individuals and the faith community to which we belong are full of human imperfections. Openness to the community and a willingness to strive after its ideals are more important than success in attaining these ideals.

One chaplain commented that many a young Catholic's difficulties with his Church really boiled down to an inability to attain the ideals of sexual conduct upheld by the Church. This, of course, is an especially pressing problem immediately prior to marriage. The person needs to honestly assess the source of his difficulties. Perhaps, when these goals of sexual conduct are no longer a problem, other difficulties of faith will lessen too. Basically there is a great need for self-understanding and self-acceptance in these areas. After accepting ourselves with our human failings we may be more able to accept God and the religious community in which we find ourselves.

Many young Christians come to marriage with varying levels of alienation, yet their relationship to the Christian community can only be on a religious level. For the Jew things are different. Judaism is a religion, a tradition, a culture, a nationality, and even a political stance. You cannot consistently be an atheistic Christian, but there are many young Jews so alienated from Judaism as a religion that they profess to be atheists. Yet they consider themselves very Jewish and are often prouder of their Jewishness than the Christian is of his Christianity. Even the atheistic Jew is proud of his Jewish heritage, tradition, and culture; he may very well be willing to fight for the political existence of Israel. This Jewish pride is very remarkable. A pride in Judaism is well founded, but only if one retains a religious bond with the community. One can be proud of being Jewish because God has chosen to work with and through the people of Israel. If one divorces God from the situation, one person has no more reason to be proud of being Jewish than another has of being Irish, Polish or Italian. This religious alienation of the young Jew bespeaks a serious problem of contemporary Judaism, but it may make religious harmony within an interfaith marriage easier. We shall see more on this later.

Conversion?

Conversion is a question that frequently arises when a couple is preparing for an interfaith marriage. As we stated earlier, a common religious belief is a strong foundation upon which a stable marriage can be built. Yet conversions merely for family unity are to be avoided. Conversion should be considered only if the person is convinced of some great lack within his own religious tradition and through study and new religious experience comes to the conclusion that a surer way of serving God can be found in another religion. If conversion comes, let it be true conversion and not mere convenience.

Without this inner conviction of the higher worth of the religion to which a person is converting, the fact of conversion may cause difficulties later in married life. The party who converts can always hold over the other party the fact that they gave up even their religion to marry him or her. This sets the other party up as almost owing something to the party that converted for the marriage.

Sometimes the question comes up of converting to a third religion, like Unitarianism. This is undesirable for the same reasons mentioned above. It puts both parties in the position of making an unnecessary sacrifice of what should be very dear to them and is not likely to deepen the religious sense of the home. A weak Christian and an alienated Jew are not likely to establish a committed Unitarian family. In entering an interfaith marriage the parties need not sacrifice all their religious differences; they need not discard their differences while only maintaining a vague belief in some sort of a transcendent being. They can each gain and share more by being as faithful as possible to each of their religious traditions.

Some will treat conversion lightly because they feel it's merely an accident of birth that they happen to be Christians or Jews. They are what they are because their parents were of that faith. They would have been Moslems if their parents were Moslems. We can't much argue with this. But isn't it more reasonable to try to be as good at whatever you are as you can? Psychologically one is better off developing his roots rather than cutting them off. We should highly value the religious community in which we were born, just because it's ours. Not that we despise any other, just that we value our own. We don't despise other families, nationalities, or countries when we value our own; it need be no different with our religion. The religion of this new family will be strengthened to the degree that each is faithful to and shares his or her religious tradition with the other.

Some people may have a subconscious desire to change religions just for the sake of change, the grass always looking greener on the other side of the fence. Others may have a latent desire to spite their parents or people associated with their religious beliefs, like a rabbi, priest, nun, or minister who did not form a pleasant part of their earlier life. Others may feel a new religion is needed to establish their own identity. None of these seem especially good reasons for conversion. It would seem much more mature and sensible to value and be good at what you are. An important part of being good at what you are may very well entail a deep and critical examination of one's faith.

Previously the Catholic party in interfaith marriages was encouraged to work for conversion of the non-Catholic. This emphasis is no longer present as the Catholic community has grown to see the inherent worth of other religious communities.

Faith of the Children

Only after the parties have come to an understanding of their own positions in each of their faith communities can the question of the religious upbringing of the children come up. The Catholic and the Jewish communities are especially concerned about the children born of their members. For some Protestant Christian communities this is not so acute a problem.

The Catholic community's concern is based upon theological principles. These principles would not be accepted by people who are not Catholics. But if we accept them just for the sake of discussion it becomes easier to understand the concern of the community.

Catholics believe that Jesus was God's Son, equal to the Father in all things. They believe that he founded a community of believers to which he wanted men to belong. The Catholic community believes that it is the continuation of this community founded by Jesus, so it is concerned that children born of its members are raised within this community.

This does not say that the Church thinks she is perfect or has an exclusive franchise on the grace of God. She also believes that God does work in other religious communities.

The Catholic community puts a few extra hurdles before an interfaith marriage than before a marriage between two of her members. The advantage of this is that it helps the couple to face the question of their difference of beliefs and how it will affect their marriage. It gives them the opportunity to get together with a priest to discuss their religious beliefs. The couple certainly should also search out a sympathetic rabbi with whom they can discuss their beliefs.

Previously the non-Catholic had to sign the much discussed "promises" which were negative in tone and simply stated non-interference with the Catholic's practice of his faith and the sharing of his faith with their children. When the party felt uncomfortable with the signing of a piece of paper to this effect, he could orally give his word, the oral word having as much weight as a signature. In either case a person's word was given.

Now the non-Catholic only has to be informed of the Catholic's responsibilities along this line and the Catholic is asked to sign or orally give his word that he will continue to practice his faith and transmit this faith to his children. The actual wording of this statement is as follows: "Realizing the gift of my Catholic Faith, I intend to use all in my power to share the Faith I have received with our children, by having them baptized and reared as Catholics."

The statement does not say that the Catholic will in fact have the children baptized and reared as Catholics, though this is obviously the intended goal. The state-

ment says that the Catholic will do all in his power to
share his Faith. It is conceivable that a conflict may
arise between the continuing stability of the marriage
and the fulfillment of this declaration. In case of such a
conflict, the stability of the marriage would naturally
have preference over the religious upbringing of the
children. It would, however, seem advisable that if the
non-Catholic party intended to make a big issue over
the religious upbringing of the children, this issue
should be raised before the marriage.

The non-Catholic party was never asked to care for
the Catholic upbringing of the children, to sign them
over to the Catholic or to bow out of having anything
to do with their religious formation. In fact both parties
should impart all they can of their religious tradition to
the children. Despite the fact that the non-Catholic
party is not asked to give any specific assurance that he
will impart his religious beliefs to the children, he obviously has a natural responsibility to impart to his
children his deepest beliefs and values. He would be
shirking his parental duties if he did not impart these
beliefs and values. The problem of both parties sharing
their faith with the children is lessened to the extent
that we realize how Christianity and Judaism can complement each other. The children can hardly suffer
from too much of an exposure to religious beliefs and
practices; they may very well suffer from too little exposure to them.

Often there is a greater resistance to interfaith marriages in the Jewish than in the Christian community.
Orthodox Jews actually go into mourning when one of
their members marries outside of Judaism. Frequently
the Christian is asked to convert to Judaism before
marriage. Even most Reform rabbis will not witness in-

terfaith marriages. The sensitivity is based upon the fear that the identity of the Jewish community will be lost through amalgamation into the majority Christian community in the United States. It may be difficult for a non-Jew to understand this sensitivity. He can more clearly appreciate it to the extent that he understands the centrality of the concept of identity as a people in the Jewish faith and the historical struggles that have taken place to maintain this identity. Christians may also be helped to understand this sensitivity if they imagine themselves as a minority religion in a country that was predominantly Jewish; in this situation they too would likely be very concerned about loss of their identity through intermarriage.

One author threw some light on the problem of maintaining Jewish identity when he observed that if one understands all the trials, wars, and purges of history through which God has preserved the people whom he has chosen, he should not be too frightened that God will allow this people to lose its identity through interfaith marriage.

How does one resolve this problem of the religious upbringing of the children in light of the sensitivities of each faith? If both parties are extremely strong in their faith, the problem is not likely to arise at all. If they are very strong in their faith, they will feel it important to marry someone who shares this faith with them. For them faith will be a significant criterion in determining with whom they develop a deep personal relationship.

Just to state a fact without making any value judgment on it, few people in our melting pot society are this committed to their faith. Even very deeply committed people do not see the religion of their future spouse as being that important. Many young people in fact find it difficult to understand why a difference in faith should present any problems in married life.

In dating, the question of faith usually doesn't even arise early in the relationship. When it does arise the person is likely already very well aware of the many good qualities in the person whom he is dating. Religion is then seen as not making that big a difference.

Both partners in an interfaith marriage should be encouraged to commit themselves as deeply as possible to their religious traditions, to share these traditions with each other and to impart these traditions to their children. In light of this, what about official initiation into the community of faith? What about the brith? What about Baptism? What about Bar or Bas Mitzvahs and Confirmation?

From a Christian viewpoint we must admit that if the two faiths can complement rather than contradict each other, so can the two rites. Christianity does not see itself as negating anything of Judaism. The first Christians in fact entered Christianity only through Judaism. They were initiated into Judaism and later into Christianity. In fact Peter and Paul had a bit of a confrontation over whether a person had to come into Christianity through Judaism. They decided not to require this, but nowhere is it forbidden. If the Christian community was founded by Jewish Christians, there can certainly be nothing inherently inconsistent with that concept even now. There is nothing of the faith of Israel that a Christian must deny, so why can't he be initiated into that faith? There is nothing of the *mitzvah* or law that a Christian must deny, so why can't he or she be considered a son or daughter of the *mitzvah*? Jews would most certainly have problems with the child being initiated into the Christian community, but

Christians need have no problem with initiation into the Jewish community. Some within the Jewish community may not consider a baptized person to be a Jew. But if there is room within Judaism even for the atheistic Jew, to be consistent there should be room for the Christian Jew as well.

At times a certain tension may exist between what a person feels he is and what his community declares him to be. One's relationship to himself and to his God may at times be different from his relationship to his religious community. This is not to say that the community is unimportant. Ideally, one's relationships with himself, his God, and his religious community should coincide and reinforce each other. It's a fact of history that in the Middle Ages the Church excommunicated many people whose relationship with God was not in any way affected by this blunder of the religious institution. Today moralists and canonists are beginning to see that a divorced person may have a different relationship to his God and to his religious community. There have been and there still can be cases where the individual is right and his religious community is wrong. Admittedly, we are on very dangerous ground when the individual and his community part, but the possibility cannot be ruled out.

What about the identity of the child? Is he a Jew or a Christian? He is a Jewish Christian, just as someone else is a Polish Christian, an Irish Christian, a German Christian, or an Italian Christian.

But this means of establishing identity seems to reduce Judaism from a religion to a nationality. It need not if one emphasizes that both parties—the Jew and the Christian—can and should contribute all they can of their religion to their spouse and to their children.

This problem is made even less severe by the fact that religion is not that central in the lives of many people. The religious core of Judaism is in fact often separated from Judaism as a culture, tradition, or heritage. This is not so readily done in Christianity. If the Jewish parent is not that deeply religious, he may be perfectly content to contribute all he can of the Jewish culture, tradition, and heritage to the children. Christianity can be presented as the religious dimension of the child's life, remembering that authentic Christianity is not seen as a contradiction by a complement of Judaism.

A feeling within the Jewish community is that the children should follow the religion of the mother. Basically this is because the mother's relationship with the child is more easily substantiated. The community is always certain of the mother of the child; at times the father may not be known. On a practical level she has more contact with the child; this extended contact ordinarily gives her greater influence. This may often be the reality of the situation. But this position can let the father off too easily. It is unfortunate that we associate religion more with maternal than with paternal influence. It's a masculine cop-out to think that the raising of the children is the mother's responsibility. The father needs to reassert his role as a co-educator of the children. Despite the fact that Judaism associates the religion of the child with that of the mother, it also emphasizes the role of the father as religious educator. One of his key responsibilities is to teach the children the *torah*, the law, the religious responsibilities outlined in the Scriptures. In interfaith marriages as in marriages of a single faith, we need to emphasize the fact that both parents are responsible for the religious formation of the children. Because the father spends less time with them, the intensity and the quality of his relationship need to compensate for this reduced time.

It is completely unrealistic to wait until the children grow up to have them choose a religious community, just as it is unrealistic to wait until the children come along to face the question of their religious upbringing. The question needs to be faced squarely and honestly before the couple gets married. The children are not brainwashed, nor is their freedom impaired, if they receive a solid religious training. Evidence of this is seen in the experience of the young people preparing for marriage themselves. Even if they were raised in a home with a single religious faith, as they approach adulthood they re-examine and question many aspects of their faith; they either more deeply commit themselves to this faith or they reject it. But at least they have something to examine and question; at least they have a background of religious convictions and values which they can question and against which they can compare other convictions and values. There is little danger that when the children grow up they will not be able to question and challenge their beliefs; there is great danger that they will have no beliefs to question.

In any case, the religious convictions of the children are not likely to be any stronger than the religious convictions of their parents. The strength of the religious convictions of the couple getting married can be traced back largely to the religious influence of their parents. It is hoped that their children will be able to say the same thing.

Marriage Ceremony

Now the question arises concerning the marriage ceremony itself. Although the marriage ceremony is the high point in the life of the bride and the groom, the preparation in faith and for marriage which anticipates the ceremony will be of much more lasting influence in the lives of both parties than will the half-hour ceremony. In light of this, the question of the type of ceremony, location for the ceremony, and minister for the ceremony are somewhat secondary. Few couples probably appreciate this priority; religious leaders in their work of marriage preparation need to bring it out.

One question that arises is that of the time for the wedding. This becomes a problem in light of the Jewish observance of the Sabbath. This observance does not allow a Jew to be married from sundown Friday to sundown Saturday; this time is designated as a time of rest. Even in the rare case when the Jewish partner would not feel inclined to observe this period of rest himself, both parties should realize that its observance is an important value in the Jewish community. Most members of the Jewish community would look askance at a wedding celebrated on the Sabbath. The Christian may find it difficult to appreciate this feeling of the Jewish community. He may be helped to understand it by envisaging the possibility of a wedding on Good Friday. There would be a parallel feeling of inappropriateness in the Christian community.

When a Jew and a Protestant Christian marry, their marriage before a minister, a rabbi, or even a justice of the peace is a valid marriage as far as their religious community is concerned. The question of who will be the official witness to the marriage will depend on the depth of the relationship of each party to his religious tradition and the depth of the sensitivity of each party to the feelings of both families. In most cases this relationship and this sensitivity would probably incline the couple to seek a clergyman to witness their marriage. When the relationship and the sensitivity are deep in each partner, it would seem advisable to have a representative of each faith have a part in the wedding ceremony.

Ordinarily a Catholic is expected to be married before a priest. Most priests will be more than happy to welcome a rabbi to share the ceremony with them in the case of an interfaith marriage. The rabbi will be welcomed into the sanctuary to give the couple his blessing, address them, and lead the assembly in prayer.

The Catholic partner may also receive what is called a dispensation from the Catholic form of marriage. With this he can be validly married in the eyes of the Church before a rabbi, or even a justice of the peace when there is sufficient reason. In this case the priest may accept the invitation to be present in the temple to give a blessing, address the couple, and lead a prayer at the ceremony.

In most cases it will be easier to arrange such a ceremony in a Catholic church than in a temple because of the strong opposition to interfaith marriages on the part of most rabbis and Jewish congregations. However, there is a disadvantage to both the church and the temple. One or other family is liable to feel rather out of place in the other's house of worship. The family that is willing to go to the other's place of worship is to be highly commended. There is no sound reason why a Catholic should feel that ill at ease in a temple or a Jew in a church. The openness that either family can show at this time will go a long way toward laying a harmonious relationship for their son or daughter and the future spouse and will no doubt draw them much closer to the family of the open-minded parents.

Some couples may feel that a home or a garden would be a fitting place for a wedding ceremony. There is certainly no denying the beauties of nature or the dignity of the home as a place of prayer. For the Jewish community the home is especially emphasized as a place for prayer. The solemn Passover season is home-oriented.

Both homes and gardens, however, leave something to be desired as far as suitable places for weddings. Marriage is a public giving of two people to each other. It has a significance not only for two families but for the total community. This communal dimension of marriage is more clearly symbolized when the wedding takes place in the gathering place of the religious community—the church or temple. The wedding of two members of religious communities in a place other than a gathering place of a religious community may actually convey a connotation of animosity to and alienation from the religious communities.

When it is available, a neutral interfaith chapel is an ideal setting for such a marriage. Both families can feel perfectly comfortable there and the bride and groom are freed of the fear of making anyone uncomfortable at their wedding. Frequently these chapels are found on college campuses.

Some catering establishments also have chapels. The great disadvantage of a wedding at the catering establishment is that the religious significance of the wedding is usually blurred. The wedding ceremony itself just becomes a part of the often gaudy bash managed by the catering establishment. Occasionally the ceremony is inserted between the cocktail hour and the dinner, diminishing both the solemnity of the ceremony and the sobriety of the congregants. The ceremony is the very reason for the celebration; therefore it deserves its own significance. Clergymen must also be cautious about too close an association with these catering establishments, lest the establishment use their willingness to assist couples entering interfaith marriages as a come-on to elicit business for themselves. It is not unheard of for such an establishment to offer a complete wedding service, including clergy—for a price of course. Most clergy would not want to be associated with such commercialism.

Present regulations within the Catholic Church look askance at a repetition of the ceremony, getting married first in front of one minister and then before another. Such an arrangement blurs the union being established between both parties. It exaggerates their separateness and the separateness of their beliefs when unity should be the theme of the day.

This unity is not even sufficiently emphasized when one minister witnesses the ceremony and the other is invited to say a few words, give a blessing, and lead a prayer afterward, for one party will feel that he is getting married before a religious leader other than his own. The gesture is not even terribly ecumenical. In effect one minister is saying to the other, "Now that I have things all tied up, you can put in your two cents."

What is needed is a fully integrated, interfaith ceremony. Present Catholic regulations are ambiguous concerning combined ceremonies. The reason for this hesitation has never been made clear. It seems that the intent of the regulations is to discourage a repetition of ceremonies either simultaneously or some time later. The development of a truly ecumenical ceremony is actually encouraged. Such a ceremony is certainly in

keeping with the prevalent spirit of interfaith cooperation today. An experimental model for such an ecumenical ceremony is found in another chapter of this book.

In planning the wedding, both parties need to be
especially sensitive to the feelings of the other and the
other's family. It would show a complete lack of sensitivity for the Catholic party to request a wedding Mass
when entering an interfaith marriage. The Jewish party
also needs to display this sensitivity by not demanding
the observance of all the Jewish wedding customs. The
custom of getting married under a floral canopy may
be one that need not be insisted upon.

However, many other Jewish wedding practices actually enhance the ceremony greatly. The custom of both
parents escorting their son or daughter down the aisle is
a beautiful expression of family unity, as is the custom
of having both parents and grandparents standing
around the bride and groom during the wedding ceremony. The ritual of sharing the cups of wine to signify
the sharing of both joy and sorrow by the married couple is also most meaningful. The breaking of the glass
at the conclusion of the ceremony has been interpreted
as merely a superstitious practice to keep away evil
spirits from the newly married couple. It also has specifically Jewish significance in recalling the sadness at the
destruction of the temple even at this most happy moment. However, it can have a deep significance even for
an interfaith marriage if it is seen as a symbolic expression of hope that the love of the bride and groom might
last until the pieces of this shattered glass come together—forever.

Some young couples might ask, "Why bother with a
wedding ceremony at all? Why not just commit ourselves to each other privately?" Such an attitude denies

the whole social nature of marriage. It has been described as equivalently saying, "I love you and commit myself to you, but I don't want anybody to know about it."

Moral Question in Marriage

It may be well worth our while now to consider the similarities and differences between Jewish and Christian moral values concerning marriage. We mentioned earlier that there was agreement that sex is good and that its deepest expression in the act of intercourse is most authentic only within the married state.

Orthodox Judaism so emphasizes the goodness of sex that a married couple is urged to enhance the Sabbath celebration by engaging in the marriage act on Friday nights.

Young people may find it difficult to appreciate the convictions of their religious communities about premarital sex. But we need to honestly realize that the human animal is both rational and rationalizing. The pleasure God has attached to human sexuality increases the likelihood of our rationalizing our morality in this area. The guidance of our religious community may help us avoid this. It is easy to say, "We have taken all precautions; this can do no harm." But one gets a completely different view when as a religious counselor he has to try to piece together lives that have been severely jarred because of a pregnancy out of wedlock or because the person who claimed so ardently that he loved the other has picked up and left. Sex is cheapened by its enjoyment without the basis of love. It is so difficult even in marriage to have two people totally and completely give themselves to each other that its practical impossibility outside of marriage seems perfectly evident. Frequently young people's concern about physical union before and even in marriage hides the deeper problem of the melding of two personalities. The development of the psychological relationship is much more important than the development of the physical; it is only the psychological merging that gives meaning to the physical act.

On family limitation, Orthodox Judaism teaches that it is moral for the woman to use birth control, but not the man. This position is based on the rabbinic interpretation that when the Scriptures give a positive command to be fulfilled during a limited space of time, this command applies only to the male. The command to increase and multiply is such a command. Reform Judaism sees no moral problem for either the husband or the wife in practicing birth control.

The problem of birth control is often viewed as a specifically Catholic moral problem. But we need to realize that the need to limit families has been most keenly felt only within the past few decades. In a largely rural society with a high infant mortality rate, the more children a family could have the better. A large family was everyone's ideal. The parents needed every set of hands possible on the farm.

Now our society is vastly different: new values and new needs have arisen. Parents are called not only to be generous, but to be responsible in the number of children they have. Drawing the narrow line of generous responsibility is a difficult task indeed.

No Catholic moralist has a problem with the principle of family limitation or child spacing. Physical, economic, psychological, educational, and social factors all contribute to the reasons for limiting a family. The Catholic community is divided as to the morality of the means used to attain this limitation.

Rhythm is accepted by all moralists as a legitimate means to avoid conception. Its legitimacy is based on the fact that it does not interfere with the natural reproductive cycle; it does not infringe upon the integrity of the individual marriage act. When the woman's cycle is not regular enough to practice rhythm, the pill can be used to regularize the cycle. The prime intention here is to regularize the cycle; the secondary effect is to inhibit conception.

Thus far there is no difference of opinion among Catholic moralists. The difference arises on whether the pill or any other means may be used with the prime intention of making conception impossible. The traditional opinion responded in the negative on the basis of the integrity of the individual marriage act and on the principle of the primary and secondary ends of marriage—the primary end being the procreation and education of children, and the secondary end being the expression of love between husband and wife.

These ends of marriage have constantly been on the seesaw over the past few decades: at one time one is stressed, at another time another, and still again both together. Interestingly, Vatican II does not even use the labels primary and secondary when discussing the ends of marriage. Even granting procreation and education of children as the primary end of marriage, the question can become academic. The practice of rhythm might create so much tension for the husband and wife as to undermine the harmony needed in the home for the education and development of the children. The use of other means of family limitation might then be necessitated even to attain what for the sake of discussion we call the primary end of marriage.

The traditional position is challenged by those who consider the total orientation of the couple toward accepting the responsibilities of parenthood more important than the integrity of the particular marriage act. The problem of rapidly increasing populations also raises questions and values that have not been raised before. The ability of a land to support additional people needs to be weighed with a couple's desire for children. A couple could have a responsibility to limit their children to two or three, even if as a family they could support more.

The English lay theologian and mother of ten, Rosemary Haughton, has an interesting interpretation of *Humanae Vitae*. She says this encyclical which deals with birth control expounds an ideal. It would be great if husbands and wives could share the wonderful gift of life without any restraint. It would also be great if a person could tell the whole and absolute truth all the time. However, we may often have to compromise these ideals. You just can't tell a woman that her new dress looks horrible or her dinner ought to be fed to the dog. So too, the human limitations of individual persons, families, or nations make it impossible to attain the ideal of a limitless sharing of life.

Protestant Christianity does not relate to a tradition of well worked out positions on the morality of birth control, abortion, divorce, or any other moral problem. Its emphasis has been more on the person than on the morality or immorality of specific acts. Protestantism has been more situation oriented than Catholicism. It has emphasized salvation more as God's free gift rather than as a payment for man's good actions; consequently, it has not emphasized the morality of specific actions as much as Catholics have.

Orthodox Judaism has a general prohibition against abortion, but it does permit it under certain circumstances. Reform Judaism does not see it as a moral problem.

Abortion is opposed by many people in different religious traditions, but the Catholic tradition is most clearly set against it. Within this moral tradition, abortion is seen as a much more serious problem than just another method of birth control. The sacredness of an already developing life adds new seriousness to the question of preventing conception in the first place.

Unlike the question of birth control where we receive ambivalent guidelines from the Catholic community, the abortion issue presents a solid consensus of opinion, saying that it is immoral under any circumstances. The basic reason is a high concern for human life. Even if we cannot establish precisely when human life begins, the fertilized ovum is only directed toward an independent human existence. It is, therefore, most sacred and deserving of care. There are always more humane ways of solving problems of pregnancy. Despite the many reasons adduced for allowing abortions, the main one in practice seems to be that the child is unwanted. In the present situation there are thousands of families wanting to adopt children. Religious and governmental institutions could easily use their influence to make the adoption of children an even greater priority in the lives of their members.

Pregnant women also need to find supportive and understanding counselors to help them cope with the natural negative feelings that accompany certain stages of pregnancy. Helped through these difficult weeks, they can come to value the life they are developing. The unfortunate association of "unwanted pregnancy" with "abortion" is a rather sad comment on the moral climate of our society.

Divorce, though not an ideal, is allowed by all branches of Judaism. The dissolution of a true and existing marriage with the right to remarry is not allowed in the Catholic community. This prohibition is based on the nature of the marriage contract, "until death," and on the social need for family stability. This permanent aspect of marriage should encourage young people to make this commitment only after very mature deliberation. Some social and psychological forces are at work that might make young people less inclined to take marriage preparation as seriously as they should. Psychologically some are still in the stage of maturing which causes them to throw off previous ties in an effort to establish their own individuality. They resent parents, religious leaders and teachers "telling them what to do." Our society also projects the image of love and marriage as something which just happens naturally. The soaring rate of marriage breakdown should quickly challenge this concept. Adults certainly don't tell each other what to do, but a mature adult also realizes that though he is the master of his own decisions he can profit immeasurably by the insight he might be able to receive from others. This insight can be culled through reading or attending seminars, classes, or conferences on marriage. It probably wouldn't be a bad idea if our civil law demanded some type of preparation before a couple could get a marriage license. We demand preparation for a hunting and driving license. Certainly marriage is more important and more laden with problems and difficulties than either hunting or driving. But, whether required or not, the couple ought to do all they can to prepare themselves seriously for marriage.

Within the marriage itself the couple should realize that a loving relationship does not just happen, nor does it just happen to dissolve. If love is to grow, it must be worked at; each party may have many sacrifices to make in order for this love to grow. When problems which the parties realize are bigger than they themselves can solve begin to arise, they should without hesitation seek the guidance of their religious leader or a marriage counselor. If we are physically sick we go to a doctor; we don't just sit there and wait for death. With no less ease and naturalness should married couples seek assistance in marriage problems.

Lack of communication has always been seen as one of the main sources of marriage difficulties. An organization called The Marriage Encounter has had fabulous success in helping couples establish a pattern of communication and dialogue throughout their married life. The Marriage Encounter is for ordinary marriages; it is not a last resort for problem marriages. It is also not an exercise in group dynamics such as the encounters we often read about. The only dynamics involved in the weekend is the dynamic of dialogue between the husband and wife. They each reflect upon their feelings on a certain topic and then exchange the reflections with each other. It is the most worthwhile way a young married couple can spend a weekend. It has taken very strong root on the East coast, but is rapidly spreading from there to other parts of the country.

The male often shows the greatest resistance to preparing for marriage, getting professional help within marriage, or taking advantage of such supportive programs as The Marriage Encounter. He more than the female feels he has all the answers and can solve all the problems he might face. On the other hand, the woman might frequently exaggerate problems. But both the man and the woman, out of love for each other, should be open to receive all the support they can before or after their wedding.

Couples involved in interfaith marriages need to be wary of joking about each other's faith. This may be an unconscious attempt to really hurt the other. It's easy to get away with hurting another in a joke or wise-crack. One can make his point, yet still hold open the escape hatch by saying he was only kidding. It might be a good ground rule for a marriage to try to avoid such cracks about each other's family or faith. If a couple find themselves tossing such barbs at each other, they should try to analyze why they are trying to hurt one another. If they can come up with the reason for this hostility, they might much more profitably discuss it right in the open, rather than hiding behind sly remarks.

As an interfaith marriage may be weakened by jokes and wise-cracks, there are unique ways in which it may be strengthened. As was pointed out earlier, the marriage can be strengthened if each party respects the faith of the other and tries to share his own faith with the other. Any person and any marriage stands to be further strengthened through worship in community. An individual who does not worship with a community may feel he is still a good person. He can rarely say that not worshiping is making him a better person. The same will hold for a couple's love in marriage. A couple which does not take worship that seriously may have a very good marriage. It would be difficult to surmise how worshiping together couldn't make their marriage even better. The Christian and the Jewish partners in a marriage should not only feel free but should be encouraged to strengthen their love through praying together at church or temple.

They can also extend their praying together into working together in civic as well as religious organizations and projects. Rather than one getting involved in the temple and the other in the church, they both might get involved in programs. They might have to work somewhat against the present structure of the religious institution to do this. Frequently religious organizations are set up for "married singles"—the men's clubs and the women's organizations. This actually works against family stability. Couples should make the extra effort to find things they can do together. The resulting effect on bringing them closer together will make the initial effort well worthwhile.

Authentic love has a way of spreading itself out. The love of a family should overflow even beyond the home. Children can be formed into much more loving personalities if they experience their parents' love for each other overflowing onto them and beyond them to those in need in their broader family or in the community in which they live. With this they can experience that love is just as much something we give as something we receive. In fact, in giving it they may well find their desire to receive it is automatically sated. The home should not so much be an island to which people run for a loving experience as a launch pad from which loving people are propelled into the world around them.

This brings up a whole area of moral problems not usually associated with married life. Most of the time moral problems of family life are limited to questions like birth control, abortion, divorce. We don't usually associate the whole sphere of social morality with family life. Yet many of these questions are faced more by couples than by individuals. What is the morality of restrictive housing covenants? What is the morality of zoning regulations which excludes from a community a balanced share of low income housing and housing for the elderly? What is the morality of our society perpetuating ghetto slums? What is the morality of financing an educational system through local taxes, thus continuing gross inequalities in funds available for education? What is the morality of clubs and organizations that bar members because of race? What is the morality of a tax system that drains family income to kill rather than develop life? What is the morality of individual families amassing more wealth than they could possibly utilize while other families lack the bare essentials of life? What is the morality of a nation which wastes more than most people have to consume? All these are moral issues that are faced largely in a family context. But even the religious institutions from which we would look for guidance on moral issues often tread much too lightly in these areas. Many times the immediate social situation in which these questions are raised is extremely complex. One cannot present ready-made answers to these questions. But we should certainly be aware of the moral dimension of these issues.

II
To Parents and
Religious Leaders

Through marriage two people join their lives together and intensify their efforts to develop their relationship of love. It is a truism to say that this is not an easy task. It can be made easier if the couple find examples and models of loving persons in their parents and their religious leaders: in those to whom they are closest and in those to whom they legitimately look for leadership in the moral life.

As has been pointed out an interfaith marriage creates special difficulties for the development of this love, so there is an even greater need for the young couple to find understanding, support, and love in their parents and religious leaders. Unfortunately this is not always the case.

To the Rubensteins and the O'Briens

Parents have turned their sons and daughters out of their home for marrying outside their faith. Clergymen have castigated couples who came to them seeking advice and help in planning their marriage. Many react with coldness and hostility to the couple—to this couple who need more attention and understanding than the couple marrying within the faith. Many religious leaders will not make the extra effort to cooperate with each other in planning an interfaith ceremony. They treat the whole question of marriage more from the viewpoint of preconceived notions rather than the needs of an individual couple.

It is one thing to be opposed to interfaith marriages in principle and to express the opposition and the reasons for it as forcefully as possible. But when a son or daughter or a member of a congregation is planning on marrying someone of another faith, we are no longer dealing in principles. Then all the opposition we can muster is not likely to dissuade the couple from carrying through their marriage. Why then run the risk of turning these young people away from their families and their religious communities?

Parents frequently feel a natural resistance to whomever their son or daughter decides to marry. They not only have an initial negative reaction to the person their son or daughter intends to marry, but they feel some opposition to the very fact of their son or daughter getting married. If couples only got married when everyone thought they were ready for marriage, we wouldn't have any marriages at all. It is difficult to let go of those we love and marriage is one more step in letting go of a son or daughter. We hear of Ever-ready batteries; often parents think of Never-ready children. Many parents also feel that no boy is ever good enough for their daughter, and no girl for their son. Parents need to remember that it is their son or daughter who is choosing a marriage partner, not they. They already had their chance and probably had the same resistance to their choice as they are giving their children.

What is frequently going through the minds of

parents and religious leaders when faced with an impending marriage is the happiness of the two people; they are concerned about whether this marriage will work out and last. After just a little experience in marriage preparation, you learn to stop asking that question. The marriages you thought would never work out do so wonderfully. And the couple you thought were meant for each other end up having a difficult time adjusting to each other. You learn that you just can't pick them beforehand.

At times a parent may not like what his son or daughter is doing. At other times he may be absolutely morally opposed to the action of his offspring. In most cases interfaith marriage would fall into the former category. But even when a child is doing something that the parent sees as absolutely wrong, parents need to ask what is the most effective way of showing their opposition.

Such a case might be if a Catholic son or daughter is marrying a divorced person, or is getting married outside the Church without obtaining the needed dispensations. The first step for the parents is to indicate their opposition with all the strength possible so that their son or daughter will have no doubt about their moral position. They can further try to talk them into changing their minds. But what do they do when it becomes obvious that their son's or daughter's mind is made up? Then the question to be asked is how the parents can do the most good for their son or daughter. Will it do more good to completely alienate them from the parents or to keep on good terms? Will it do more good to cut them off from the family completely or to maintain a loving relationship with them? Will it do more good to refuse to attend the wedding or to attend it and keep communication open? These questions are not always easy to answer. But love rather than vindictiveness must be the guide. The old adage about more flies with a spoonful of honey than with a barrel of vinegar applies here.

The hostility to interfaith marriage is often stronger with Jews than with Christians. Often there is a fear of losing a member of the Jewish community. Often this fear can be allayed by encouraging the Jewish partner to maintain even stronger ties with his community before marriage than after. The more strongly he is committed to Judaism, the more of the Jewish tradition he can share with his spouse and children. Through the Jewish partner the spouse and children can be more favorably exposed to the cause of Judaism than they could if they married within their own faith. Thus not only are the parents gaining a son or daughter, but Judaism is gaining a sympathetic Gentile.

Christian parents can also see the positive side of an interfaith marriage in that their children and grandchildren will have a chance to be exposed to the fullest understanding of Christianity through the Jewish partner. Through their understanding of God's working with the people of Israel as seen in the Jewish Scriptures, they will know more of God's working with them.

Parents of both faiths need to react to their future son- or daughter-in-law as a person. The first question they should ask is, "What kind of person is my son or daughter planning on marrying?" They should not allow their religious prejudices to blind them to the personal qualities of someone of a different faith.

The couple and their parents might profitably be aware of the somewhat different emphasis the Jewish and Christian traditions place on the wedding ceremony and the wedding celebration. While certainly not being turned off to celebrations, the Christian puts a great deal of emphasis on the wedding ceremony. For a valid marriage, a Catholic must ordinarily be married in a religious ceremony. The festivities celebrate the main event of the day—the exchange of vows by the couple. The Jewish tradition often puts more emphasis on the celebration. The Jewish partner can be validly married in a civil ceremony. Sometimes the ceremony is almost lost between the cocktail hour and the dinner. Families need to be sensitive to each other on this matter.

Often parents feel there will be a gap between them and their grandchildren if their son or daughter marries outside his or her faith. They can be reassured by knowing that the grandchildren will not be raised in one tradition or the other, but in both traditions.

Most young people are more than considerate of the feelings of their parents as they prepare for marriage. But some parents become downright obnoxious in meddling in their son's or daughter's life at this point. Parents can make their desires and concerns known, but they should let the couple themselves make the decisions as to the format of the ceremony, the upbringing of the children, etc. The clergyman can usually most effectively work with the couple themselves, and, using the insights outlined earlier, work out a truly harmonious relationship. Things always get unnecessarily complicated when parents get embroiled in the situation. However, a sympathetic clergyman may be effective in putting apprehensive parents a little more at ease. They may well be in a better position to communicate with the parents than the couple are. Communication between clergy and parents usually begins with neutral or even positive feelings, whereas the couple and their parents may be communicating with a whole background of negative feelings.

Religious Leaders

It would be most helpful for clergy to see the opportunity of preparing a couple for marriage as an opportunity to prepare them for adult faith as well. The marriage preparation will, perhaps, be the most extensive amount of time these young adults will spend with their religious leaders. Often young people come to marriage with a child's perception of their faith. Their education in other areas far surpasses their religious knowledge and experience. It's little wonder, then, that they have problems of faith.

When the parties preparing for marriage are of the same faith, one can occasionally complement the perception of the other. When they are of different faiths, this is not possible. Yet to the degree that they appreciate and are at ease with their own religious tradition, they can share this tradition with their spouse and children.

The priest or minister should not presume that the only one needing to be made familiar with Christian teaching and practice is the non-Christian. The non-Christian may lack information; the Christian himself may often be misinformed, and have more serious problems because of this misinformation. The same presumption is likely true for the rabbi on the Jewish side.

Both the Christian minister and the rabbi should work with both parties to lay the foundation for an adult faith. Each should in fact recommend that the couple visit the other and discuss questions of faith with him. Frequently a conversation on problems of faith can be launched by asking the couple if they have gotten into any discussions on religious topics. It is certainly of a high priority to discuss any religious areas of friction with the couple.

Many couples complain that their religious leaders are more interested in the faith of their children than they are in the faith of the couple. We may be able to get an assurance, a promise, or a signature concerning the religious formation of the children, but what good will this be if the parents have serious unresolved problems with their religious communities? All this will take time, but at what point in the life of a member of the congregation could a clergyman's time better be spent than when this member is embarking on a new path in life? It is at the time of marriage that decisions will be made which will affect the lives not only of the couple but of the whole new family. If the religious leaders through their openness and concern can favorably dispose these young people to their religious communities, they are likely making it easier for them to relate to the one God to whom these communities themselves are directed. This God who was open to the people of Israel even in their farthest wanderings, this Christ who is open with forgiveness to his followers even in their gravest faults, should be reflected in the openness of the clergy. It is expected that some clerical readers will disagree with some of the particular viewpoints or practical suggestions contained in this work. But it is hoped that this disagreement will not hinder the development of a generally more open, loving attitude toward couples planning to marry outside their faith.

Official Policy

The priest works in much more of a hierarchial structure than the minister or rabbi. He is more responsible to the policy of the diocese, whereas the rabbi is more responsible to the feelings of his congregation. Both should utilize all the freedom they have in dealing with interfaith marriages. The rabbi may be able to influence the thinking of his congregation to a greater understanding of interfaith marriages. The priest, through the latest policies drawn up by the U.S. Conference of Catholic Bishops, has a very full range of possibilities within which to work with interfaith marriages. He should not be more confining in his own personal attitudes than is the official Church. Where the Church leaves leeway, as a minister of the Church the priest is hardly justified in limiting that leeway. General regulations make it easy to obtain a dispensation from the form of marriage. Where reasons indicate, the priest should quickly recognize these reasons and apply for the dispensation. He should also make himself available to witness the ceremony along with the rabbi.

Not only the individual priest, but local diocesan policy as well, must be as open as the general regulations. Diocesan officials should realize that the priest dealing with the couple is in a far better position to determine the type of ceremony, the minister of the ceremony, and the location of the ceremony than is some chancery official.

It should be presumed that the priest is working with a value system regarding the best ceremony, minister, location, etc. He has to relate this system of priorities to the individual couple with whom he is working. When he requests permission for a wedding in a catering establishment, a garden, or whatever, it should be presumed that he is doing so because, all things considered, it does not seem advisable to have the wedding in a church or temple.

Serious questions arise concerning not only the legality but the morality of some diocesan policies. A major east coast archdiocese with a large Jewish population adamantly refuses to grant a dispensation from the form of marriage if the wedding is not going to take place in a church or temple. As pointed out earlier, the church or the temple may put one or other family ill at ease. Does not a dispensation from the form really mean that the couple is free from the regulations of the Church as far as minister, location, and ceremony are concerned? One presumes that this policy is adopted to prevent having weddings at restaurants, gardens, and seashores. But again, the common sense of the priest working with the couple should be presumed. Canonically there seems little justification for withholding the dispensation from the form on the basis of the location of the wedding; if the reasons for the dispensation are valid, it must be granted without restrictions.

The very morality of this situation is open to question. The policy has forced couples to be married invalidly. Yet even when the chancery was presented with the certainty of this invalid marriage, they refused to grant the dispensation. Within their categories this is equivalent to telling the couple to go and live in sin for a while before getting a revalidation of the marriage. In reality, if there is any sin involved, it is certainly not on the part of the couple.

It was pointed out earlier that both the Catholic and the Jewish partner have a natural responsibility as parents not only to feed, clothe, house, and educate their children, but also to instill in them their highest values and the system of beliefs that provides meaning for their lives—their faith. The Catholic community asks for a formal commitment to this responsibility from its members. It would be good if the Jewish community had the same expectation, i.e., asked its members who enter an interfaith marriage to give a formal assurance that they would continue their contact with the Jewish community and would impart an appreciation and practice of this faith to their children.

Judaism, being less hierarchically and authoritatively structured than Catholicism, is not likely to adopt this as an official policy. Individual rabbis might, however, consider this approach to interfaith marriages. Catholic bishops and chanceries might also take the leadership and ask priests to obtain such an assurance from the non-Catholic party. Provision for it might even be made a part of the form requesting a dispensation from the disparity of cult marital impediment. The point to be re-emphasized here is that the family is not as likely to suffer from an excessive exposure to either faith as it is to suffer from a lack of faith.

Marriage Preparation

Most religious leaders tear their garments asunder at the rising rate of marriage breakdown in our country. Yet it is religious leaders who have the greatest contact with couples before marriage. There is a serious lacuna in our pastoral programs where we are not providing a quality preparation for marriage. Within the Jewish and Protestant traditions marriage preparation is pretty much contained in a couple's private conversations with the clergyman. The Catholic tradition has the pre-Cana movement—one, two or three group sessions addressed by a married couple, priest, and doctor.

Could not priests, ministers and rabbis in a given area pool their resources and tap the resources of psychologists, sociologists, marriage counselors, and married couples to present a more intensified marriage preparation program?

One such program is underway at the Interfaith Chapel of C. W. Post College on Long Island in New York. It is an eight-week series of marriage preparation for engaged couples. Its approach is strictly non-denominational so that two Jews, two Catholics, two Protestants, two atheists, or any mixture thereof might feel comfortable. Its goal is strictly quality marriage preparation. The following are the topics covered in their eight sessions:

1. Why marriage? — An approach to the pressures in our society toward marriage; an attempt to discover what each partner is bringing to their particular marriage; an approach to healthy and unhealthy motives people have in getting married. Given by a professional marriage counselor.

2. What is love? — An examination into how it grows, can break down, and is expressed; an examination of many of the ideas of Eric Fromm on love. Given by a clergyman and a married couple.

3. Human physiology — A gynecologist-obstetrician discusses the physical aspect of human sexuality.

4. Psychology of the sexes — A psychologist discusses male and female differences in attitudes, expectations, needs.

5. Communication in marriage discussed by a married couple.

6. Moral values — An open discussion with a rabbi, priest, and minister on pre-marital sex, birth control, abortions, interfaith marriages, divorce, social questions.

7. Marriage breakdown — A divorce lawyer discusses the genesis, evolution, and solution of serious marital problems.

8. Toward a happy home — A married couple discuss finance, in-laws, friends, priorities, and other concrete practical questions of married life.

This particular seminar runs on a continuous basis every eight weeks. Each evening's discussion is independent of any other one, so that nothing mentioned in a previous session is presupposed in a later session. This is done so that couples may start attending the seminar anywhere along the line; they may take a few sessions at one time and make up the ones they missed the next time around. This is a realistic approach to the realities of conflicting commitments in the lives of the couples.[1]

This program has been found most effective in preparing couples for marriage. A modified program like this might even be practical for newly married couples. Couples in which one party was away at school or in the service before marriage might more conveniently avail themselves of such a program after they are married.

---

[1] Further information on this seminar may be obtained by contacting the author of this book at C.W. Post College Chapel, Greenvale, N.Y. 11548.

III
Inter-Marriage: A Jewish View

Rabbi Bernard M. Zlotowitz

Judaism is opposed to inter-marriage, i.e., the marriage between a Jew and a non-Jew, on religious grounds.[1] The Central Conference of American Rabbis reflects this view in a resolution passed in convention assembled in New York City in 1909 and reaffirmed in 1947. "The C.C.A.R. declares that mixed marriages are contrary to the tradition of the Jewish religion and should, therefore, be discouraged by the American Rabbinate."

This attitude is not readily traceable to the Biblical period but is derived from the Rabbinic period. The Bible enumerates definite prohibitions against marriage with certain peoples.

"You shall not make marriages with them (the Hittites, the Girgashites, the Amorites, the Canaanites, the Perizzites, the Hivites, and the Jebusites), giving your daughters to their sons or taking their daughters for your sons." (Dt. 7:3)

"For they would turn away your sons from following me, to serve other gods; then the anger of the Lord

[1]Note: Marriage to a convert to Judaism is not regarded as an inter-marriage. Such a person is a Jew in every respect.

would be kindled against you, and he should destroy you quickly." (Dt. 7:4)

However, it countenances inter-marriage with people other than from these groups: Joseph married an Egyptian woman and Moses married the daughter of Jethro, a priest of Midian, and later takes to wife a Cushite woman. David married Batsheva, the widow of Uriah, the Hittite and Solomon had the proverbial one thousand wives outstanding among whom was an Egyptian princess. Esther married a non-Jew, Ahaseurus. It is only later that the prohibition against marrying outside of the Jewish faith is expanded by Ezra and Nehemiah to include all non-Jews.

"And Ezra the priest stood up and said to them, 'You have trespassed and married foreign women, and so increased the guilt of Israel. Now then make confession to the Lord the God of your fathers and do his will; separate yourselves from the peoples of the land and from the foreign wives.' "(Ezra 10:10-11 cf. Neh. 10:31)

Ruth represents the bridge between the Biblical attitude and the Rabbinic one.[2] Ruth is the first convert to Judaism recorded in the Bible. Her first husband was Mahlon, a Jew, whom she married in the land of Moab and her second husband was Boaz whom she married in the land of Judea. Between her first and second marriage, Ruth converted to Judaism, reflecting the transition of the taboo against marrying outside of the faith. Ruth personifies the two attitudes. Marriage outside of the faith is still acceptable when she married for the

---

[2]Though the Bible places Ruth in the period of the Judges all Biblical scholars are agreed that it was written at the time of Ezra and Nehemiah, 5th century B.C.

first time. However, by the time of her second marriage, the law is firmly established that marriage outside of the faith is not permitted.

The Rabbis were especially concerned with preserving Jewish group identity. For them, the family played a major role in the process of group preservation. Opposition to marriages between Jews and non-Jews was not only upheld, enforced and reaffirmed by the Rabbis throughout the ages, but the Church also vigorously opposed and forbade such unions (the Council of Elvira about 300 A.D. forbade marriage between Christian girls and non-Catholics; Innocent III decreed through the Fourth Lateran Council—1215—that Jews wear distinctive garb. Innocent's reason for separating Jews from Christians was that it prevented inter-marriage).

The modern Jew no less than the ancient and medieval Jew held similar views. When Napoleon I convened a Jewish Synod (Sanhedrin) in 1807 he put several questions to this august body. One question dealt with inter-marriage. The answer is an historic one: "The great Sanhedrin declares that marriage between Israelites and Christians contracted according to the laws of the Civil Code are binding and civilly valid, and although it is not sanctioned by religious forms, it will not involve any anathema."[3] And where marriages were so contracted they were not sanctioned or solemnized by the Rabbis. Even the general Jewish community viewed with disdain such marriages. In fact, such a

---

[3]"Le grand Sanhédrin déclare en outre, que les mariages entre israélites et chrétiens contractés conformément aux lois du Code Civil, sont obligatoires et valables civilement et que, bien qu' ils ne soient pas susceptibles d' être revetus des formes religieuses, ils n entraineront aucun anathéme."

marriage was an anathema to the family contrary to the decision of the Napoleonic Sanhedrin. They would observe *shivah*, i.e., mourning rites for a person entering such a union. For all intents and purposes he was dead—cut off from the living Jewish community.

The Jewish community no longer takes such a harsh view of inter-marriage nor would a family observe *shivah* today (except among the ultra-orthodox). However, the vast majority of the Jewish community still does everything in its power to discourage such a marriage. Dr. David Einhorn, one of the foremost Reform Rabbis of the 19th century, was so vehement in his opposition to inter-marriage that he declared: "Such marriages are to be strictly prohibited even from the standpoint of Reform Judaism."

In order to understand the traditional Jewish attitude two things should be clear. Firstly, the Jew is a minority group and he wishes to preserve the historic identity of his people for which his forebears gave their lives and were martyred. According to statistics cited by the American Jewish Year Book (1963) and several others, e.g., Werner J. Cahnman, "Intermarriage and Jewish Life" (1963), seventy-five per cent of the children of inter-married couples are not brought up as Jews; and even where the children remain nominally Jewish the traditions are not observed. In short, inter-marriage makes for a dilution of Jewish solidarity. Or in the words of Dr. Einhorn again: "To lend a hand to the sanctification of mixed marriage is, according to my firm conviction, to furnish a nail to the coffin of the Small Jewish Race with its sublime mission." Rabbis are committed to safeguarding the group identity of the Jewish people and, therefore, do not officiate at such marriages[4] and thus preside over the weakening of the bonds that unite the Jewish people. Whereas a certain amount of inter-marriage is inevitable when Jews and Christians live side by side, those Rabbis who willingly officiate at such marriages give their imprimatur and would speed the process of the assimilation of the Jew.

Secondly, there is another important consideration. Judaism is a legalistic religion, i.e., it is a religion governed by a legal discipline. Marriage is the fulfillment of a legal ritual—it is a contractual relationship. It is not a sacrament as in the Roman Catholic Church and certain Protestant denominations. Like any legal contract both parties must subscribe to the basic tenets of the contract in order to make it legal. How then can a non-Jew subscribe to the formula of Jewish marriage—"ha-ray at m'koodeshet . . . behold thou art consecrated unto me with this ring in accordance with *the law of Moses and of Israel*"—when he doesn't believe in the teachings of Judaism? Thus for all intents and purposes he cannot legally enter into such a contractual relationship. Such a marriage is not a Jewishly sanctified one.

Though Reform Judaism advocates a liberal approach to religion, it does not at all imply favoring inter-marriage. Opposition to inter-marriage is in no way a denial of equality. Every group has a basic right to self-preservation. The ideal in America is for a pluralistic society. True liberalism recognizes such pluralism and does not pursue the old concept of the melting pot. True liberalism is the right to live in a mo-

---

[4] I am fully aware that there are some Reform Rabbis that do officiate at such marriages but they are in the minority.

saic where each group continues to develop its individual cultures and religious beliefs to the enhancement of each group and to the enrichment of the whole society.

I recognize that one cannot prevent inter-marriage altogether, and statistics show a trend upward. However, there are some deterrents which could be pursued. I don't believe that the answer lies only with formal education. It has to do with developing a Jewish life style which makes one feel his Jewish identity viscerally and emotionally as well as intellectually. This is achieved not necessarily in the classroom of the Jewish Religious School but in the home—in a living Jewish community as well as in the Temple. It means that our young people have to be exposed to Jewish experiences so that they get to feel "Jewish." It is natural that when one selects a mate he does not want her to be too different. This Jewish feeling must be transmitted to our young people. How to expose them to these Jewish experiences becomes the challenge of the synagogue and home working together. A camp devoted to Jewish living and visiting Israel are but two suggestions. Any experience that will create a meaningful living Jewish life style is the key to the making of a positive Jew.

IV
Christian-Jewish
Wedding Ceremony

*This combined ceremony is offered on an ex-
perimental basis. It shows how it is possible to
integrally combine both rites. It is the work of
the late Rabbi Samuel Halevi Baron, Revs.
Ronald Luka, C.M.F. and Gregory Kenny,
C.M.F., and Professor Robert McAfee Brown. It
appears to be a lengthy ceremony. This presentation contains many options which will not
be used in an actual ceremony, which should
take no longer than a half hour.*

I. INTRODUCTION (Priest or Rabbi)

Every marriage ceremony is a unique event because, even if the same words are used, the couples are never the same, and a unique set of circumstances has brought together two unique
human beings. But added to all of that today is the
fact that, in this particular marriage, not only are
two human beings brought together, but two faiths
as well. This means that parts of the service will be
familiar to Jews but not to Christians, and other
parts will be familiar to Christians but not to Jews.

And just as neither _____ nor _____ will be asked, after their marriage, to surrender what is real and vital in their respective faiths, no more in the service that unites them today should we suppress what is real and vital out of either of these two ancient traditions. Thus, to take the point of greatest possible misunderstanding, if the Christian is not asked to suppress the name of Christ, no more is the Jew asked to affirm that name. Each is asked only to be faithful to what is highest to him or her.

_____ and _____, in the very ceremony that unites you today you are expressing your intent to be faithful to each of your religious traditions. By the very fact of asking both a rabbi and a priest to witness your exchange of vows, you are asking us to join you in expressing to your families and friends the fact that each of you considers your religious tradition to be important. In marriage you are not sacrificing your commitment to these traditions but reaffirming it and promising to share it with one another and with your children. Remember the religious context in which you begin your marriage today and live lives consistent with that context in the years ahead (Rev. Ronald Luka).

Christians and Jews have not had a good record of association over the centuries. No Jew needs to be told that bit of understatement; some Christians need to be reminded of it. It is therefore all the more significant that Jews and Christians gather here today, sharing much of a common religious heritage, and sharing totally in a common humanity we often forget we have, *not* to be further divided, but to be drawn even closer to one another, as we celebrate the joining together of the lives of _____ and _____. Their marriage, beyond all that it means to them of the human love of man and woman for one another, is for them and for us in addition a foretaste of the breaching of past human misunderstanding and mistrust between two groups of people, and the pledge of a new future for all men, which their marriage helps inaugurate, in which suspicion is replaced by trust, and hatred by love. This is the dawn of a new tomorrow. It is indeed the day which the Lord has made. Let us rejoice and be glad in it (Robert McAfee Brown).

II. INVOCATION

Verses of Invocation and Thanksgiving:

Rabbi: (a) *Barukh habbah b'shem Adonoy; Berakhnukhem mibbeth Adonoy.*

Priest: Blessed is he who comes in the name of the LORD.
We bless you from the house of the LORD. Ps. 118:26.

Rabbi: (b) *Mi addir al hakkol, mi barukh al hakkol, mi gadol al hakkol; Hu y'bharekh eth hechathan w'eth hakkallah.*

                    (Hebrew Prayerbook)

Priest: May he who is almighty, he who is all-blessed, he who is exalted above all, bless this bride and bridegroom!

Rabbi: (c) *Barukh ettah, Adonoy Elohenu, Melekh ha-olam, She-he-che-yanu w'q'iy'manu w'higgiyanu laz'man hazzeh.*

Priest: Praised be Thou, O Lord our God, Ruler of the Universe, who hath granted us life, and hath sustained us, and hath brought us to this happy and auspicious occasion (*Hebrew Prayerbook*).

Rabbi: (d) *Zeh hayyom asah Adonoy; nagilah w'nism'chah bho.*

Priest: This is the day the LORD has made; Let us be glad and rejoice in it. Ps. 118:24.

III. SCRIPTURE READINGS

A large and exhaustive selection of readings is presented here. The clergymen and the couple can select a few which they find most meaningful. The couple may also wish to here introduce some secular literature which has a special significance for them. It would seem appropriate, however, to keep religious insights on love and marriage predominant in that this is a religious ceremony. Several of the following passages may be read by the priest and/or rabbi.

As we prepare for the solemn and joyful moment when _____ and _____ exchange their marriage vows, it would be good for us to reflect thoughtfully on the Hebrew and Christian Scriptures apropos of love and marriage:

God created man in his image; in the divine image he created him; male and female he created them. God blessed them saying: "Be fertile and multiply; fill the earth and subdue it." Gen. 1:27f.

So the LORD God cast a deep sleep on the man, and while he was asleep, he took out one of his ribs and closed up its place with flesh. The LORD God then built up into a woman the rib that he had taken from the man. When he brought her to the man, the man said: "This one at last is bone of my bones and flesh of my flesh; this one shall be called 'woman,' for out of 'her man' this one has been taken." That is why a man leaves his father and mother and clings to his wife, and the two of them become one body. Gen. 2:21-24.

But Ruth said, "Do not ask me to abandon or foresake you! For wherever you go I will go, wherever you lodge I will lodge, your people shall be my people, and your God my God. Wherever you die I will die, and there be buried. May the LORD do so and so to me, and more besides, if aught but death separates me from you!" Ruth 1:16f.

When the girl's parents left the bedroom and closed the door behind them, Tobiah arose from bed and said to his wife, "My love, get up. Let us pray and beg our Lord to have mercy on us and grant us deliverance." She got up, and they started to pray and beg that deliverance might be theirs. He began with these words:

"Blessed are you, O God of our fathers; praised be your name forever and ever. Let the heavens and all your creation praise you forever. You made Adam and you gave him his wife Eve to be his help and support; and from these two the human race descended. You said, 'It is not good for the man to be alone; let us make him a partner like himself.' Now, Lord, you know that I take this wife of mine not because of lust, but for a noble purpose. Call down your mercy on me and on her and allow us to live together to a happy old age."

They said together, "Amen, amen," and went to bed for the night. Tobit 8:4-9.

Grandchildren are the crown of old men, and the glory of children is their parentage. Prov. 17:6.

He who finds a wife finds happiness; it is a favor he receives from the LORD. Prov. 18:22.

When one finds a worthy wife, her value is far beyond pearls. Her husband, entrusting his heart to her, has an unfailing prize. She brings him good, and not evil, all the days of her life.

She reaches out her hands to the poor, and extends her arms to the needy. She fears not the snow for her household; all her charges are doubly clothed.

She is clothed with strength and dignity, and she laughs at the days to come. She opens her mouth in wisdom, and on her tongue is kindly counsel.

Her children rise up and praise her; her husband, too, extols her: "Many are the women of proven worth, but you have excelled them all." Charm is deceptive and beauty fleeting; the woman who fears the LORD is to be praised. Prov. 31:10-12, 20f., 25f., 28-30.

Hark! my lover—here he comes springing across the mountains, leaping across the hills. My lover is like a gazelle or a young stag. Here he stands behind our wall, gazing through the windows, peering through the latices. My lover speaks; he says to me, "Arise, my beloved, my beautiful one, and come! . . . O my dove in the clefts of the rock, in the secret recesses of the cliff, let me see you, let me hear your voice, for your voice is sweet and you are lovely." My lover belongs to me and I to him. Cant. 2:8-10, 14, 16a.

For stern as death is love, relentless as the nether world is devotion; its flames are a blazing fire. Deep waters cannot quench love, nor floods sweep it away. Were one to offer all he owns to purchase love, he would be roundly mocked. Cant. 8:6f.

Happy the husband of a good wife, twice-lengthened are his days; a worthy wife brings joy to her husband, peaceful and full is his life. A good wife is a generous gift bestowed upon him who fears the LORD. Be he rich or poor, his heart is content, and a smile is ever on his face.

Like the sun rising in the LORD's heavens, the beauty of a virtuous wife is the radiance of her home. Like the light which shines above the holy lampstand are her beauty of face and graceful figure. Golden columns on silver bases are her shapely limbs and steady feet. Sir. 26:1-4, 16-18.

Some Pharisees came to him and said, to test him, "May a man divorce his wife for any reason whatever?" He replied, "Have you not read that at the beginning the Creator made them male and female and declared, 'For this reason a man shall leave his father and mother and cling to his wife, and the two shall become as one'? Thus they are no longer two but one flesh. Therefore, let no man separate what God has joined." Mt. 19:3-6.

Jesus began to address them, once more using parables: "The reign of God may be likened to a king who gave a wedding banquet for his son." Mt. 22:1f.

One of them . . . asked him, "Teacher, which commandment of the law is the greatest?" Jesus said to him: " 'You shall love the Lord your God with your whole heart, with your whole soul, and with all your mind.' This is the greatest and first commandment. The second is like it: 'You shall love your neighbor as yourself.' On these two commandments the whole law is based, and the prophets as well." Mt. 22:35-40.

On the third day there was a wedding at Cana in Galilee, and the mother of Jesus was there. Jesus and his disciples had likewise been invited to the celebration. Jn. 2:1f.

If I speak with human tongues and angelic as well, but do not have love, I am a noisy gong, a clanging cymbal. If I have the gift of prophecy and, with full knowledge, comprehend all mysteries, if I have faith great enough to move mountains, but have not love, I am nothing. If I give everything I have to feed the poor and hand over my body to be burned, but have not love, I am nothing.

Love is patient; love is kind. Love is not jealous, it does not put on airs, it is not snobbish. Love is never rude, it is not self-seeking, it is not prone to anger; neither does it brood over injuries. Love does not rejoice in what is wrong but rejoices in the truth. There is no limit to love's forbearance, to its trust, its hope, its power to endure. Love never fails. 1 Cor. 13:1-8.

In any case, each one should love his wife as he loves himself, the wife for her part showing respect for her husband. Eph. 5:33.

Beloved, let us love one another because love is of God; everyone who loves is begotten of God and has knowledge of God. The man without love has known nothing of God, for God is love. 1 Jn. 4:7f.

IV. EXHORTATION OR HOMILY

*Here the priest, minister, or rabbi may want to
give a homily drawn from the sacred text ex-
plaining the dignity of wedded love or the responsibilities of married people, keeping in
mind the circumstances of the particular marriage. Two possible themes are developed
here.*

_____ and _____, as you know, you are about to
enter into a union which is most sacred and most
serious, a union which was established by God
himself. By it, he gave to man a share in the greatest work of Creation, the work of the continuation
of the human race. And in this way he sanctified
human love and enabled man and woman to help
each other live as children of God, by sharing a
common life under his fatherly care.

Because God himself is thus its author, marriage is
of its very nature a holy institution, requiring of
those who enter into it a complete and unreserved
giving of self. . . .

This union then is most serious, because it will bind
you together for life in a relationship so close and
so intimate that it will profoundly influence your
whole future. That future, with its hopes and disap-
pointments, its successes and its failures, its plea-
sures and its pains, its joys and its sorrows, is hid-
den from your eyes. You know that these elements
are mingled in every life and are to be expected in
your own. And so, not knowing what is before you,
you take each other for better or for worse, for

richer or for poorer, in sickness and in health, until death.

Truly, then, these words are most serious. It is a beautiful tribute to your undoubted faith in each other, that, recognizing their full import, you are nevertheless so willing and ready to pronounce them. And because these words involve such solemn obligations, it is most fitting that you rest the security of your wedded life upon the great principle of self-sacrifice. And so you begin your married life by the voluntary and complete surrender of your individual lives in the interest of that deeper and wider life which you are to have in common. Henceforth you belong entirely to each other; you will be one in mind, one in heart, and one in affections. And whatever sacrifices you may hereafter be required to make to preserve this common life, always make them generously. Sacrifice is usually difficult and irksome. Only love can make it easy; and perfect love can make it a joy. We are willing to give in proportion as we love. And when love is perfect, the sacrifice is complete.

No greater blessing can come to your married life than pure conjugal love, loyal and true to the end. May, then, this love with which you join your hands and hearts today never fail, but grow deeper and stronger as the years go on. And if true love and the unselfish spirit of perfect sacrifice guide your every action, you can expect the greatest measure of earthly happiness that may be allotted to man in this vale of tears. The rest is in the hands of God.
—Catholic Ritual

OR:

_____and _____, I am not going to preach a sermon or give you a fearsome "charge," but I am going to remind you briefly of one of the themes taken from the first lesson from the Hebrew Scriptures, Scriptures later taken up and appropriated by the Christian community as well. You will recall that in the Creation story there is the refrain after each act of creation, "And God saw that it was good." But after the sixth day, the day of the creation of male and female (which I have always thought was one of the better days), the refrain is intensified: "And God saw that it was *very* good."

What the two of you represent today, the love of man and woman, is looked upon as the very peak and purpose of Creation, with the whole of the created order as the arena or stage upon which the drama of human love can be enacted. So what we are celebrating today is nothing less than the very best thing there is.

There is a second thing the Creation story tells us: It tells us that man is made in the image of God, that the clearest reflection of what God is like is to be found not in rocks or trees or hillsides but in human beings. But it goes on to say something about the location of that divine image that is often overlooked. For the Genesis account continues, "In the image of God he created him, male and female he created them."

In other words, you don't discern the image of God

when you have a solitary human being; you discern the image of God when you have human community, and most particularly the community of male and female. It is not in either of you alone, but in the two of you together, that the rest of us this day discern where God is most closely present in our midst.

And this means a third thing: that the two of you will receive your own definition not separately, but together.

Who is _____? From today on, he is _____ only as _____ and _____.
Who is _____? From today on, she is _____ only as _____ and _____.

Neither of you is any longer complete without the other; neither of you can be understood by us, or can understand each other, save by reference to the other. God will be present in your lives, and through your lives to your friends, to the degree that you truly mirror his image in the full communion of your totally shared lives. And you will deface his image, and your own, to the degree that you deny or ignore this indissolubility that henceforth will define who you are.

To which I add a final thing, not contained in the Creation story, but an important implication of it. We live in a world where men ceaselessly deny the divine image implanted in them. To the degree that we continue to deny it, we bring about our own destruction, and the destruction not only of those we hate but also of those we love. One of the most blatant denials of that image has been the enmity between Jews and Christians. There has been hatred and rancor and spite and almost everything else between Christians and Jews—almost everything else except love. Your marriage is a small and yet gigantic step in the reversal of that trend; for here you are, a Christian and a Jew, declaring in the most public and binding way your love for one another. That puts a special burden, and a special glory, upon your marriage. For your marriage becomes a sign, a very precious sign, that nothing—not even 2,000 years of enmity—is stronger than love; and you offer to all of us a living reminder, through the whole of your marriage, that the way you have chosen is the way we must choose; and that just as through your love you affirm the image of God in mankind, so we too, through our love for one another, can affirm that image, not only in ourselves, not only in those we love, but wonderfully even in those we are only now beginning to come to know.

So we thank you for that. You are already giving each of us a great gift; and I pray that throughout the whole of your marriage you can multiply to all who know you, a thousand-fold, the greatness of that gift. — Robert McAfee Brown

V. PRAYERS OF INTERCESSION

This is an optional part of the ceremony which may be led by either of the ministers or shared

by both. To each intention the congregation is asked to respond, "Lord, hear our prayer."

O God, we believe that you are the Creator of the world, of man, of all of us, and of _____ and _____, who will shortly join their lives in your love. We believe that you did not abandon us after creation, but continue to reveal yourself to us in your words and in your deeds. We believe that you love us and want us to love you and each other, and so we ask you:

That all men may grow in love, respect, and understanding of each other, let us pray to the Lord. LORD, HEAR OUR PRAYER.

That Christians and Jews might generously respond to the love you have shown for them by loving each other and being a sign of your love for man, let us pray to the Lord. LORD, HEAR OUR PRAYER.

That the love with which _____ and _____ bind themselves together today may grow deeper and broader throughout their married life, let us pray to the Lord. LORD, HEAR OUR PRAYER.

That among their families and friends _____ and _____ might find an outstanding ideal in marital love, let us pray to the Lord. LORD, HEAR OUR PRAYER.

God, our Father, we ask you to hear and answer these prayers and all the prayers, hopes, and aspirations within each of our hearts, especially within the hearts of _____ and _____. Answer these prayers, we beg you, according to your loving and provident will.

VI. EXCHANGE OF VOWS

> *Priest:*   _____ and _____, have you come here freely and without reservation to give yourselves to each other in marriage?
>
> Will you love and honor each other as man and wife for the rest of your lives?
>
> Will you accept children lovingly from God and bring them up according to his law?

Priest or rabbi, to whichever party happens to be of his faith:

> _____, wilt thou have this woman to thy wedded wife, to live together after God's ordinance in the holy state of Matrimony? Wilt thou love her, comfort her, honor her, and keep her in sickness and in health; and, forsaking all others, keep thee only unto her, so long as ye both shall live?

> *Groom:*   I will.

OR

_____, do you take _____ to be your wife? Do you promise to be true to her in good times and in bad, in sickness and in health, to love her and honor her all the days of your life?

Groom: I do.

_____, wilt thou have this man to thy wedded husband, to live together after God's ordinance in the holy state of Matrimony? Wilt thou love him, comfort him, honor him, and keep him in sickness and in health; and, forsaking all others, keep thee only unto him, so long as ye both shall live.

Bride: I will.

OR

_____, do you take _____ to be your husband? Do you promise to be true to him in good times and in bad, in sickness and in health, to love him and honor him all the days of your life?

Bride: I do.

Then turning towards each other, looking at each other and clasping each other's hands, the bride and groom repeat after the priest or rabbi:

Groom: I, _____, take thee, _____, to my wedded wife, to have and to hold from this day forward, for better for worse, for richer for poorer, in sickness and in health, to love and to cherish, till death us do part, according to God's holy ordinance; and thereto I plight thee my troth.

OR

I, _____, take you, _____, to be my wife. I promise to be true to you in good times and in bad, in sickness and in health. I will love you and honor you all the days of my life.

Bride: I, _____, take thee, _____, to my wedded husband, to have and to hold from this day forward, for better for worse, for richer for poorer, in sickness and in health, to love and to cherish, till death do us part, according to God's holy ordinance; and thereto I plight thee my troth.

OR

I, _____, take you, _____, to be my husband. I promise to be true to you in good times and in bad, in sickness and in health. I will love you and honor you all the days of my life.

Alternate forms for the exchange of vows may be found in Appendix A.

VII. BLESSING AND EXCHANGE OF RINGS

The priest blesses the rings with one of the suggested formulae. The rabbi then leads the Jewish party in the Hebrew and English formula for the exchange. The Christian minister then leads the Christian party in an adaptation of that same formula.

May the Lord bless these rings which you give each other as a sign of your love and fidelity.

OR

Lord, bless these rings which we bless in your name. Grant that those who wear them may always have a deep faith in each other. May they do your will and always live together in peace, good will, and love.

OR

Lord, bless and consecrate _____ and _____ in their love for each other. May these rings be a symbol of true faith in each other and always remind them of their love.

[For Jewish Party] Hareh at (attah) m'quddesheth m'quddash li b'tabba-ath zu k'dath Mosheh w'Yisra-ehl:

With this ring I thee wed. Behold, be thou consecrated unto me by this ring as my wife (husband), in accordance with the faith of Judaism (Christian faith) and the law of God and man.

VIII. DOUBLE WINE CEREMONY
   (led by the rabbi)

(a) Barukh attah, Adonoy Elohenu, Melekh ha-olam,
Boreh p'ri haggaphen.

Praised be Thou, O Lord our God, Ruler of the universe,
Creator of the fruit of the vine. (Hebrew Prayerbook)

Let the cup of wine which you are now about to drink in common symbolize the joys of life that you are divinely destined to share with one another as the years go by. God grant that you drink deeply together of the cup of joy.

(Both Bride and Groom partake)

This cup of wine is connected by Jewish tradition with the Birkhath Erusin, the preliminary benediction of Betrothal:

Barukh attah, Adonoy Elchenu, Melekh ha-olam,

Praised be Thou, O Lord our God, Ruler of the universe,
Who in Thy love dost sanctify life by the holy covenant of marriage.
(Hebrew Prayerbook)

In accordance with the divine promise as recorded in the Book of Hosea, we recall the words of that great Prophet of a God of Love—that first Prophet of a God of Love—spoken in the name of the Lord:

I will espouse you to me forever; I will espouse you

in right and in justice, in love and in mercy. I will espouse you in fidelity, and you shall know the LORD. Hos. 2:21f.

(b) But it is—alas!—the universal fate of humankind that we are born to experience sorrow and suffering as well as happiness. May you therefore, out of the great love you bear one another, no less gladly be ready and willing to bear and share each other's burdens. Drink together, then, from this second cup of wine, as a symbol of the cup of sorrow you both vow to share—and share alike—if such indeed should be the will of God.

[Both Bride and Groom partake]

This second cup of wine, and this second blessing over the wine, is associated by Jewish tradition with the Shebhah B'rakhoth l'Nissuin, the progressive sequence of Seven Benedictions of Marriage:

—Praised be Thou, O Lord our God, Ruler of the universe,
  Creator of the fruit of the vine.

—Praised be Thou, O Lord our God, Ruler of the universe,
  Who hast created all things for Thy glory.

—Praised be Thou, O Lord our God, Ruler of the universe,
  Creator of man.

—Praised be Thou, O Lord our God, Ruler of the universe,
  Who didst make man in Thine image, after Thy likeness,

and didst fashion woman to be his helpmate
evermore:
Praised be Thou, O Lord, who causest bride and
bridegroom to rejoice.

—May these, Thy children, establish a household
for the glory of Thy name:
Praised be Thou, O Lord, who lovest Thy crea-
tures.

—Praised be Thou, O Lord our God, Ruler of the
universe,
Who last created joy and gladness, love and
brotherhood, peace and fellowship.

—May it be Thy will to bring blessing upon <u>not only
the children of all Israel, but equally upon all Thy
children and upon all mankind.</u> *

—Praised be Thou, O Lord, who fills the hearts of
bride and bridegroom with joy. (Hebrew Prayerbook)

(c) _____, and_____, as you now drink in common
from one and the same cup, so may you, with
God's guidance, in fervent devotion to one another,
together draw contentment, comfort, and true feli-
city from the cup of life—and thereby find the joys
of life doubly gladdening, its sorrows sweetened
because divided in two, and all things hallowed by
complete companionship and sacred love.

(d) Clasping one another's hands together, you do
now mutually pledge yourselves to undying love in

* Underscored words added to the Hebrew original by Rabbi
S. H. Baron.

the deathless words of the lovely and loving Ruth, as recorded in our Sacred Scriptures—Scriptures sacred alike to all those who share our common Judaeo-Christian religious, ethical, and spiritual heritage:

And Ruth said unto Naomi:
"Entreat me not to leave thee, and to return from following after thee.
For whither thou goest, I will go; and where thou lodgest, I will lodge.
Thy people shall be my people, and thy God my God.
Where thou diest, will I die, and there will I be buried:
The Lord do so unto me, and more also, if aught but death part thee and me!"   Ruth 1:16-17

IX. CONFIRMATION OF THE MARRIAGE BOND

Rabbi: Inasmuch as you have both expressed the avowals that seal this bond of wedlock, therefore, in accordance with the faith of Judaism, and in conformity with the laws of the State of New York, and by virtue of the authority vested in me by this State as an ordained Rabbi, I do hereby ratify the confirmation of your marriage vows and pronounce you, _____and_____, to be lawfully wedded as husband and wife in the sight of God and man.

Priest: Forasmuch as you, _____ and _____, have consented together in holy wedlock, and therefore have pledged your faith to each other, by the authority of the Catholic Church I witness and bless the bond of marriage you have contracted.

Furthermore, I call upon all of you here present to be witness of the bond we now confirm and bless. I call upon you not only to witness this bond but by your love, by your understanding, by your friendship and compassion to work to help _____ and _____ to strengthen and develop this bond throughout their wedded life. For man must not separate what God has joined together.

THE LORD'S PRAYER [Optional]

[*Introduction: Rabbi Samuel Halevi Baron*]

The ecumenical spirit of our time goes back belatedly to the Biblical teachings—in both the Old and New Testaments—of the great Prophets of justice and righteousness, of love and forgiveness, of universal peace, of the Fatherhood of God and the brotherhood of man. That spirit is happily exemplified and prayerfully implemented in this fully integrated antiphonal jointly Judaeo-Christian marriage service.

Accordingly, it is not inappropriate that, on this occasion, both Christians and Jews should join in reciting together the Lord's Prayer, which—far from being exclusively Christian—was written down (like everything else in the New Testament) by Jewish hands. As a matter of fact, speaking as an ordained Rabbi of Liberal Judaism, I can assure my Jewish co-religionists of all shades of belief and practice and affiliation—whether Orthodox, Conservative, or Reform—that scholarly research has established the accepted existence of numerous parallels to all the parts and language of the Lord's Prayer in the Hebrew Bible, in the post-Biblical Talmudic literature, and in the medieval and modern Jewish Prayerbook. It is as Jewish a prayer as anything could be, and therefore it can now be considered a truly Judaeo-Christian prayer:

[*Priest and people together*]

Our Father, who art in heaven, hallowed be thy name, thy kingdom come, thy will be done on earth as it is in heaven.
Give us this day our daily bread;
and forgive us our trespasses
as we forgive those who trespass against us;
and lead us not into temptation,
but deliver us from evil.
For thine is the kingdom, the power,
and the glory forever and ever. AMEN.

XI. PRIEST'S CONCLUDING BENEDICTION

Almighty God our Father, for all of us the God of

Abraham, Isaac, and Jacob, and for some of us the God and Father of Jesus Christ; you who have created us, provided for us, and out of your love for _____ and _____ have assembled us together in this place:

We give you thanks for these your servants, now joined together as husband and wife, and we ask your providence and grace over their life together. As they explore their new relationship, give them gentleness and strength, power and compassion, an experience of the heights and depths, the excitement of tomorrow and the contentment of yesterday.

Help them to make their home a place where love is truly present and where all who enter can feel that there is new hope for all persons because there is love between these two persons. Help them to draw together from their previous circles of family and friends those who would not otherwise know one another, and weave through these new relationships ever stronger bonds of love and understanding. Enable them to give to their children a place where security and freedom can dwell together, where choices can be honored for their integrity, and where new possibilities offer fresh challenges.

Be with all other couples here today, our Father, and may this declaring of the vows of _____ and _____ be for them a reconfirmation of their own marriage vows and a new start in their own marriages. Be with all Jews and Christians who in the past have scorned one another, and be with all members of the human family who have despised or neglected those different from themselves, so that new bonds of concern and compassion may be forged across previously insurmountable barriers.

These things we ask, in faithfulness to our understanding of who you are, and of what is your will for us. Amen. — Robert McAfee Brown.

OR

May Almighty God, with his word of blessing, unite your hearts in the never ending bond of pure love. R. Amen.

May your children bring you happiness and may your generous love for them return to you, many times over. R. Amen.

May the peace of Christ live always in your hearts and in your home. May you have true friends to stand by you both in joy and in sorrow. May you be ready and willing to help and comfort all who come to you in need. And may the blessings promised to the compassionate be yours in abundance. R. Amen.

May you find happiness and satisfaction in your work. May daily problems never cause you undue anxiety, nor the desire for earthly possessions dominate your lives. But may your hearts' first desire be always the good things waiting for you in the life of heaven. R. Amen.

May the Lord bless you with many happy years

together, so that you may enjoy the rewards of a good life. And after you have served him loyally in his kingdom on earth, may he welcome you into his eternal Kingdom in heaven. R. Amen. — Rite of Marriage from the Roman Ritual.

OR

Remember, O Lord, our God, their parents who have reared them; for the prayers of the parents strengthen the foundations of a house.

Remember, O Lord, our God, Thy servant _____ and Thy handmaid _____, and bless them. Grant them the fruit of the womb, fair children, and the union of soul and body; exalt them as the cedars of Lebanon and as the fruitful vine, so that, having all things in sufficiency, they may abound in every work that is good and acceptable to Thee; and let them see their children's children, like olive branches around their table. And after they have pleased Thee, may they shine like stars in Thy heaven. O God, Who didst make man from clay and woman from his side, giving her to him to be his helpmate, stretch forth Thy hand once more to unite these Thy servant and Thy handmaid; for it is Thou who makest the union. Join them in unity of spirit, crown them in love, unite them in one flesh, grant them fruitfulness, so that they may be upright and rejoice in many children.

XII. THREEFOLD BENEDICTION BY THE RABBI

And with this (these) solemn and sacred declara-

tion(s), do I (we) invoke upon you the Divine Benediction, in accordance with the gracious promise
recorded in the *Torah*, the Hebrew Bible, the Holy
Scriptures, in the immortal words of the beloved
threefold Priestly Blessing, as pronounced in days
of yore in the primitive desert

(a) Y'bharekh'khah Adonoy w'yishm'rekhah:

May the Lord bless you and keep watch over
you;

(b) Ya-er Adonoy panaw elekhah wiy'chunnekkah:

May the Lord cause his face to shine upon you
and be gracious unto you;

(c) Yissah Adonoy panaw elkhah, w'yasem l'khah
shalom:

May the Lord lift up his countenance upon you
and grant you the blessings of peace (and of
health and happiness and harmony—with each
other, with your loved ones, with your fellow-
men, and with your God—now and forever-
more).
Amen.

XIII. BREAKING OF THE GLASS

Rabbi: In Jewish tradition the breaking of
the glass at a wedding symbolizes
the sorrow of the people at the destruction of the temple in Jerusalem.

It reminds us even in our moments of greatest joy.

The breaking of the glass is also a symbolic prayer and hope that your love for one another will remain until the pieces of this glass come together again.

XIV. SIGN OF PEACE

Priest: The celebration of love between a man and a woman recalls God's love for us his people and his command that we love our neighbor. The bride and groom now exchange their first kiss as husband and wife.

But the true love of a husband and a wife for each other must overflow from themselves to their families, to their children, to their friends and neighbors, especially to those in great need of their love.

As they meet their families and friends in the reception line, they not only accept your congratulations but extend their love to you.

APPENDIX — ALTERNATE FORMS OF CONSENT

WEDDING CREED AND VOWS

**Bride
and
Groom:** We believe that by our love we bear witness to the union of God and his people.

We believe that we are meant to be for each other a sign of God's love.

We believe that we are called to bring each other to God.

We believe that we are called to build up the family of God here on earth.

We believe that we are meant to give our children in service to God and mankind.

Groom: I accept you as my wife and call upon the Jewish and Christian Communities to witness our union.

Both: With the witness of these Communities, we offer ourselves together as man and wife to God.

Witnesses: We have heard _____ and _____ pledge themselves to each other and to God in marriage. Before God and

84

these Communities, we testify that
_____ and _____ are now husband
and wife, one flesh.

OR

**Priest
or
Rabbi:**
_____, wilt thou have this Woman to
be thy wife, and wilt thou pledge thy
troth to her, in all love and honor, in
all duty and service, in all faith and
tenderness, to live with her, and
cherish her, according to the ordinance of God, in the holy bond of
marriage?

Groom: I will.

**Priest
or
Rabbi:**
_____, wilt thou have this Man to be
thy husband, and wilt thou pledge
thy troth to him, in all love and honor,
in all duty and service, in all faith and
tenderness, to live with him, and
cherish him, according to the ordinance of God, in the holy bond of
marriage?

Bride: I will.

Groom: I,_____, take thee,_____, to be my
wedded wife; And I do promise and
covenant, Before God and these witnesses, To be thy loving and faithful
husband, In plenty and in want, In joy
and in sorrow, In sickness and in
health, As long as we both shall live.

Bride: I,_____, take thee,_____, To be my wedded husband; And I do promise and covenant, Before God and these witnesses, To be thy loving and faithful wife, In plenty and In want, In joy and in sorrow, In sickness and in health, As long as we both shall live.

Suggested Readings

The titles below have been found to be helpful in providing an adult grasp of Judaism and Christianity for the party of that respective faith and for his or her intended spouse.

On Judaism

Donin, Hayim Halevy. *To Be a Jew:* a Guide to Jewish Observance in Contemporary Life. New York: Basic Books, Inc., 1972.

Kertzer, Morris. *What Is a Jew?* New York: Macmillan.

Steinberg, Milton. *Basic Judaism.* New York: Harcourt, Brace, Jovanovich.

Zlotowitz, Bernard. "Folkways and *Minhagim,*" reprinted from *Keeping Posted.* New York: Union of American Hebrew Congregations.

On Christianity

A New Catechism. New York: Herder and Herder. This is a translation of the Dutch Catechism and contains the very latest of scriptural and theological scholarship on an adult level. Catholics should not let the title scare them away. The book is not more of: "Who made you? God made you. . . ."

Greeley, Andrew. *A Future to Hope in.* New York: Doubleday, 1969. Explores some of the questions with which modern man daily wrestles and some of the insights Christian beliefs can bring to these questions.

Luka, Ronald, C.M.F. *Hangups in Religion.* Chicago: Claretian Publications, 1970. Explores many of the questions and problems young Catholics have with their faith.

Wilhelm, Anthony J., C.S.P. *Christ among Us:* A Modern Presentation of the Catholic Faith. Paramus: Paulist Press, 1972.

About the Author

Father Luka holds a licentiate in theology and a master's in sociology from the Catholic University of America. He subsequently pursued studies toward a doctorate in sociology at the University of Chicago. He has been a college chaplain for the past eight years at C.W. Post College, the State University of New York at Farmingdale, and the New York Institute of Technology, all on Long Island. During the past year, 35 out of the 50 marriages he witnessed at the Interfaith Chapel of C.W. Post College were interfaith.

2-802